Sympathetic Realism

BOYANOSKI

Sympathetic Realism

GEORGE A. REID AND THE ACADEMIC TRADITION

Art Gallery of Ontario
Musée des beaux-arts de l'Ontario

Front cover:

42 George A. Reid
The Berry Pickers 1890
Oil on canvas
Government of Ontario Art Collection,
Toronto

Canadian Cataloguing in Publication Data

Boyanoski, Christine, 1955 —
  "Sympathetic realism": George A. Reid and the
academic tradition

Catalogue for an exhibition held at the Art Gallery
of Ontario, Aug. 22-Oct. 19, 1986.
Bibliography: p.
ISBN 0-919777-33-3

1. Reid, G.A. (George Agnew), 1860-1947 — Exhibitions.
I. Reid, G.A. (George Agnew), 1860-1947.   II. Art
Gallery of Ontario.   III. Title.

ND249.R4A4 1986   759.11   C86-094310-0

The Art Gallery of Ontario is generously funded
by the Province of Ontario, Ministry of Citizen-
ship and Culture. Financial support for the
Gallery's operation is also received from the
Municipality of Metropolitan Toronto and the
Government of Canada through the Museums
Assistance Programme of the National Museums
of Canada, and the Canada Council.

Credits

Editing and Chronology: Robert Stacey

Graphic Design: Steve Boyle

Typesetting: Canadian Composition Incorporated

Colour separations: Litho Plus Inc.

Photo Credits

Wayne Barrett, Prince Edward Island: no. 2; Art
Gallery of Ontario: front cover, nos. 1, 3, 4, 5, 6,
7, 10, 11, 14, 15, 16, 18, 19, 20, 21, 22, 23, 24,
25, 26, 27, 28, 29, 30, 35, 37, 40, 41, 43, 44,
45, 48, 50, 51, 53, 54, 55, 56, 57, figs. 3, 9, 10,
11; The National Gallery of Canada: nos. 8, 31,
39, 46, 49; T.E. Moore, Toronto: nos. 9, 17, 38,
42, 47; McMaster University Art Gallery, Hamilton: no. 12; Glenbow Museum, Calgary: no.
13; Department of External Affairs, Ottawa: no.
32; Art Gallery of Hamilton: nos. 33, 34; The
Winnipeg Art Gallery: no. 36; C.W. Jefferys
Estate Archive, Toronto: fig. 1; Pennsylvania
Academy of the Fine Arts, Philadelphia: figs. 2,
8; Philadelphia Museum of Art: figs. 4, 5, 12;
Metropolitan Toronto Library: fig. 6; The Metropolitan Museum of Art, New York: fig. 7.

Lenders to the Exhibition

Art Gallery of Hamilton

Art Gallery of Ontario, Toronto

Art Gallery of Windsor

Mr. and Mrs. J. Browning, Toronto

Confederation Centre Art Gallery and Museum, Charlottetown

Glenbow Museum, Calgary

Government of Ontario Art Collection, Queen's Park, Toronto

Kaspar Gallery, Toronto

London Regional Art Gallery

McMaster University Art Gallery, Hamilton

National Gallery of Canada, Ottawa

Private Collection

Private Collection

Victoria University, University of Toronto

Winnipeg Art Gallery

Itinerary

Art Gallery of Ontario, Toronto   22 August - 19 October 1986

Thunder Bay National Exhibition   19 November - 29 December 1986
Centre, Thunder Bay

Kitchener-Waterloo Art Gallery,   15 January - 22 February 1987
Kitchener

Burlington Cultural Centre   5 - 29 March 1987

Rodman Hall Arts Centre,   10 April - 17 May 1987
St. Catharines

Acknowledgements

The initial step in organizing any exhibition is often to gather together a sufficient number of paintings of quality and interest to represent clearly the artist's oeuvre. In some cases, as when the work has fallen out of favour with contemporary audiences, many paintings have either disappeared or are in a bad state of repair due to neglect or age. While George Agnew Reid was a very prolific artist in the 1880s and '90s, a relatively small percentage of works from this period have come to light. I am therefore grateful to the lenders who have so generously loaned their works for a year of travel, and to those who have helped me locate others - in particular the Toronto auction houses of D. and J. Ritchie, Sotheby's, and Waddington's, through whose rooms have passed a number of Reid paintings over the past few years.

My research into Reid's early work was facilitated through discussions with others interested in this period, particularly Victoria Baker, Assistant Curator of Early Canadian art at the National Gallery in Ottawa, who has been organizing a major retrospective on Paul Peel, a contemporary of Reid's. Thanks are also due to Cheryl Leibold, archivist, and Jeannette Tookey, Research/Curatorial Assistant at the Pennsylvania Academy of the Fine Arts, and Darrell Sewell, Curator of American Art at the Philadelphia Museum of Art. Ms. Muriel Miller and Robert Stacey generously shared information with me, and Mrs. Pamela Bonnycastle's enthusiasm was much appreciated.

Within the Art Gallery of Ontario, the Conservation staff has been particularly helpful. Sandra Lawrence, Chief Conservator advised me on the condition of the works and suggested treatment which was carried out by Barry Briggs, Assistant Conservator, and Anita Henry. The staff of Photographic Services, especially Carlo Catenazzi, Head Photographer, and Faye van Horne, were very accommodating of my last-minute requests. Thanks are also owed to the staffs of Technical Services and Extension Services, who have been responsible for carrying out my wishes concerning the installation of the show both at the Art Gallery of Ontario and throughout the province. Alan Terakawa, Acting Head of Promotions, and Steve Boyle, Designer, are to be thanked for their contributions to producing this publication.

Finally, I am grateful for the willing and cheerful support of Leila Jamieson, Secretary to the Curator and the Assistant Curator of Canadian Historical Art.

Christine Boyanoski
Assistant Curator, Canadian Historical Art

"Sympathetic realism" was the term used in 1895 by an American writer to characterize the paintings of George Agnew Reid[1] (1860-1947). It describes his approach to painting from the late 1880s to the mid-nineties, which manifested itself in the production of large-scale genre pictures imbued with moralistic overtones. These pictures, which fell out of favour early in the twentieth century (and whose present physical condition in some cases tells of this neglect), nonetheless enjoyed great popularity in the late nineteenth century, when any artist with an eye to personal success quickly learned what would hang in the salons or annual exhibitions, and accordingly catered in an appropriate manner to contemporary taste.

Reid brought the full benefit of his artistic training in Toronto, Philadelphia and Paris to bear on his major canvases - works produced specifically for acceptance in the salons and for sale soon after. His art education was firmly rooted in the academic tradition, and although his style evolved from smooth, carefully "finished" examples to a freer, more impressionistic and, later, decorative manner, he never strayed far from it. As late as 1931, in fact, when the artist was seventy-one and the international art world had seen a rapid succession of avant-garde styles like Post-Impressionism, Cubism and Surrealism, Reid held fast to the Academic idea: he continued to believe that it should be elastic, liberal and comprehensive enough freely to adapt all the results of new investigations to its uses and that "the great academic tradition marches with stately tread along all the centuries, gathering in its train all the great and choice spirits, all the movements of proven value, every solid accomplishment and advance along technical and aesthetic lines, and that it is still doing so today."[2]

That same previously quoted writer of 1895 referred to George Reid as a "liberal-conservative" in art - an apt description of an artist in whom the academic tradition was deeply ingrained, but who nonetheless remained open in some degree to modernist experimentation. In this respect, Reid had much in common with contemporary American painters, many of whom went straight to the "source," by continuing their art studies in Paris after receiving their initial training in academies

Fig. 1
George A. Reid's Life Class, 1886-87, courtesy of C.W. Jefferys Estate Archive, Toronto. Photo by J. Fraser Bryce, Toronto. Back row, centre: C.W. Jefferys; back row, right: Owen Staples; extreme left: W.W. Alexander.

in the United States. But, by the time they reached Paris - considered to be the centre of the art world at that time - their conceptual bias was so strong that they were loath to give up the academic principles they had been taught, and most could not fully adopt the newer perceptual mode, Impressionism.[3] For these pilgrims, as for much of the art world, Edouard Manet and Puvis de Chavannes were the heroes of the day. In addition, once in Paris, they sought out *"juste milieu"* painters like Thomas Couture, Jean-Léon Gérôme or Jules Bastien-Lepage as masters; these were painters who balanced tradition with contemporaneity and were considered to be "modernizers of tradition."[4] The end result was that the North Americans, too, became eclectic painters.

George Reid's work of the last two decades of the nineteenth century demonstrates the process whereby a foreign style is transplanted in North American soil. The final product resembles neither the native original nor the foreign source with which the artist came in contact. George Reid reached the height of his eclectic style in the early 1890s; and because it is these works on which he first made his reputation and which reveal so much about what a young Canadian artist learned from external models, it is the products his early formative years that are the focus of this exhibition.

Laying the Ground

In the face of parental disapproval, George Agnew Reid pursued the interest in art that he had displayed from an early age. His father, a Scottish immigrant farmer, who settled near Wingham, Ontario, around 1840, had tried to persuade his son to become an architect, and apprenticed him to J.B. Proctor, owner of a local architectural firm, in 1878. This was all to no avail, however, and at the first opportunity the young George set out to obtain a fine-art education, inspired by the example of the venerable Seaforth, Ontario landscape painter William Nichol Cresswell (1822-88), whose studio Reid had visited in 1876.

The artistic training Reid subsequently obtained was firmly rooted in the French academic tradition as embodied in the curriculum of the

Ecole des Beaux-Arts in Paris, the most revered art institution of that period. He first came in contact with the Academic idea through his studies at the Central Ontario School of Art with Robert Harris (1849-1919), a Paris-trained Canadian artist who arrived in Toronto in 1879.

The training he received with Harris was reinforced and broadened soon after at an American art institution, the Pennsylvania Academy of the Fine Arts, into which an advanced version of the French atelier system had been introduced by Thomas Eakins (1844-1916), Director of the school from 1882 to 1886. Eakins initially had quite an impact on the young Canadian's work in terms of style and subject matter. However, the strength of this influence weakened in the face of Reid's first-hand experience of French painting at the Julian and Colarossi academies in Paris in the late 1880s and again a decade later, and of the paintings of the Spanish Baroque master Velasquez. Reid was not alone in his admiration for Velasquez, whose work enjoyed tremendous popularity in the late nineteenth century.

Reid was therefore part of this tradition, his teachers being former pupils of the academic painters Alphonse Legros and Léon Bonnat (Harris), Gérôme and Augustin Alexandre Dumont (Eakins), and he himself having been taught by Benjamin Constant, Jules-Joseph Lefebvre, Jean-Paul Laurens and William-Adolphe Bouguereau. He, in turn, passed it on to the students of his private life painting class once he set himself up in Toronto as a professional painter in 1885-6. His pupils - Owen Staples, F.S. Challener and C.W. Jefferys among others - all benefited from Reid's experience beyond narrow provincial boundaries (fig. 1).

The basis of academic art as taught at the Ecole des Beaux-Arts and of all academic criticism was the gradual mastery of the human form in a literal, naturalistic style.[5] The student would begin by drawing from antique casts and then progress to working from the living model. Before extensive reforms were made to the curriculum of the Paris Academy in 1863, this was the extent of instruction in the combined section of painting and sculpture at the Ecole des Beaux-Arts; the practical techniques of painting and sculpture would be learned in the private atelier of a master. These ateliers served as an alternative for foreign students. After 1863, the atelier system was better integrated into the official

Fig. 2
William M. Harnett
Borghese Warrior   1873
Black and white chalks, body colour
with brush
100.3 x 86.4 cm
The Pennsylvania Academy of the
Fine Arts, Gift of Mr. and Mrs. David
J. Grossman

school, but, as before, most foreign students sought their training outside the Ecole - they could not, in any event, compete for the coveted Prix de Rome, which could only be won by a French national and which was the main advantage of admission to the Ecole. Study after the antique cast and the nude living model was also the basis for instruction in the ateliers. This tradition found its way to the United States. The *Circular of the Committee of Instruction* at the Pennsylvania Academy of the Fine Arts for 1882-83, the year Reid began his studies there, stated unequivocally, "The course of study is believed to be more thorough than that of any other existing school. Its basis is the nude human figure."

Reid had had little exposure to art before enrolling in night classes at the Ontario School of Art in the winter of 1878-79. His first teachers were established members of the Ontario Society of Artists - Marmaduke Matthews, John Fraser, Henri Perré, and Charlotte Schreiber, most of whom specialized in landscape painting. He studied charcoal drawing with Lucius O'Brien, who was to become the first president of the Royal Canadian Academy in 1880. In 1879 Robert Harris began teaching at the School, taking over the antique class.

Reid won the President's medal for the "Best shaded drawing from cast (antique)" in 1880 (no. 1a). Indeed, he must have reached a high level of competence in this area by 1882, for, on his arrival at the Philadelphia Academy, rather than spend the prescribed initial six months drawing from the antique, he advanced immediately into life drawing when Thomas Eakins saw what he could do.[6] The application form for admission to the school stated, "students will be transferred from the Antique to the Life Class as soon as they have demonstrated, by their work in the Antique, their ability to profit by the Life Classwork." An early example done in Philadelphia is his rapid pen-and-ink sketch of the *Borghese Warrior* (no. 3), a plaster cast that had been drawn by countless other students in many different styles and from which students at the Academy continue to draw today. William Harnett's fine chalk drawing (fig. 2) demonstrates a high degree of academic "*fini*" by contrast to the Reid.

What benefit did the authorities of these institutions see in such prolonged and repetitive exercises based on inanimate objects? Apart

Fig. 3
Robert Harris
The Newsboy   1879
Oil on canvas
54.6 x 43.5 cm
Art Gallery of Ontario, Gift of the
Ontario Society of Artists, 1947

from exposing the student to the art of ancient Greece through copies of its finest sculpture, these casts had the advantage of being immobile, and of having a uniform colour so that the student could easily render the effects of light and shade without the added complication of flesh tones, which he or she would encounter later with the live model. Proportion and action could be taught more easily from the cast.

Another important aspect of the academic system which figures in the discussion of drawing from antique casts is that of the "copy." Just as students copied examples of antique sculpture, they were encouraged to make painstaking copies, literal reproductions, in fact, of the works of great masters in order to learn how they were made, and with the hope that these studies would capture the essence of that artist's style. Often, a good percentage of the student's income would be obtained from making copies of famous works and selling them. This they were encouraged to do by their instructors.

Two of Reid's copies are included in this exhibition: the first (no. 2) is an 1880 copy after Robert Harris's *Newsboy* (fig. 3), which had been completed in 1879. Reid's figure of the boy is less comfortably situated in the picture space than is Harris's, and his treatment is more linear; one is aware of the "outline." It is very difficult to reproduce the spontaneity of a painterly approach, though at that time Harris's style was certainly easier for Reid to copy than that of a Velasquez, with its visibly fluid and rapid brush technique, would have been. Reid did copy the works of the Spaniard in the Prado, Madrid, years later (no. 49). Harris himself commented favourably on the broad treatment and assurance displayed by Reid's copy, which earned Reid a full year's certificate for oil painting.[7] This "broad treatment," a characteristic of the new French method emphasized by Harris in his teaching, was immediately seized upon by Reid. As he explained,

> Harris taught us how to look at objects, no matter what character, as made up of a series of planes and masses which, if broadly simplified, could be

Fig. 4
Thomas Eakins
Professionals at Rehearsal   c. 1883
Oil on canvas
40.6 x 30.5 cm
Philadelphia Museum of Art, John D. McIlhenny Collection

resolved into finer and finer planes and masses until every detail could be pursued and given its proper proportion and value....

In later years, when I went to Paris to study, I recognized this as the French method, as the professors constantly used the expressions "*Les valeurs*," "*Le ton vaste*," "*Dessinée par la masse*." Draw or paint by mass and observe the exact tone or the values.[8]

In his copy of the *Newsboy*, Reid captured this planar quality most noticably in his treatment of the hands.

There was no shame in making such copies, as it was an integral part of the system. An academically trained artist, even if not making a literal copy, may have fallen back on this *modus operandi* and lifted certain motifs from works of other artist to incorporate in his own painting. Subjects and figural groupings were borrowed freely.

Reid seems to have made no copies of the work of Thomas Eakins, although some of the titles of his own contributions to exhibitions are similar to those of his master: for example, *The Rehearsal* (exhibited in 1885) and the *Zither Player* (shown in 1884 at the 12th annual exhibition of the Ontario Society of Artists) may have been Reid's own version of Eakins's *Professionals at Rehearsal* (fig. 4), a work of 1883 in which two of the American teacher's students are featured: J. Laurie Wallace, Eakins's favourite pupil, sat for the zither player, and for the guitar player, Reid himself.

Reid would also have known Eakins's sailing pictures, such as *Sailboats Racing on the Delaware*, 1874 (fig. 5), and although there are some major stylistic differences between the two works, *Toronto Bay*, 1886 (fig. 6), shows Reid exploring a similar subject in his own city. And Eakins's *Arcadia*, 1883 (fig. 7), painted at the time Reid was his student, is one of several canvases and bas-reliefs on the Arcadian theme that must surely have been in Reid's mind when he executed his *Music* in 1899-1900 (nos. 53-56) in a variety of media. Even though Reid left the Academy in 1885, he maintained contact with his *alma mater* by sending pictures to the annual exhibitions of the Pennsylvania Academy of the Fine Arts in 1886 and each year from 1890 to 1893, and continued to be interested in the career of Thomas Eakins well into the 1930s.[9]

Once the student advanced beyond drawing from the antique, he

Fig. 5
Thomas Eakins
Sailboats Racing on the Delaware
1874
Oil on canvas
61.0 x 91.4 cm
Philadelphia Museum of Art: Given
by Mrs. Thomas Eakins and Miss
Mary Adeline Williams

was then set to making *académies*, or drawings and paintings from the live model. Reid's instruction at the Ontario School of Art, which had consisted of rudimentary drawing and outline, design and copying antique casts, and drawing from objects,[10] had not given him the opportunity to work from the live nude model. An article describing the curriculum at the Pennsylvania Academy of the Fine Arts that appeared in *Scribner's Monthly* in 1879[11] captured his interest. In a 1939 letter, Reid related that

> The article described Eakins' method of teaching as having broken away from the stilted type of academic training, and the students painted without preliminary drawing, using the brush only, for all drawing, the painter and sculptor students modelling and painting together. Also that there was [*sic*] anatomy and perspective lectures, the anatomy lectures being illustrated with a dissected body prepared in the Academy dissecting room. All this appealed very strongly to me because of its radical character and thoroughness and I resolved to continued my training there.[12]

Eakins was at his most influential as a teacher at the Academy from 1882 to 1886, during which period he served as Director. What distinguished his tenure was a change of emphasis in the curriculum, which was described in the *Scribner's* article and which Reid neatly summarized in the passage quoted above. While Eakins continued in the tradition of the school by passing on the basics of French academic training to his students, he discouraged prolonged study of the antique, believing that casts were only imitations, and instead encouraged drawing with the brush. The *Circular of the Committee on Instruction* of the Pennsylvania Academy for the academic year 1883-84 stated:

Fig. 6
George A. Reid
Toronto Bay, 1886 1887
Oil on canvas
55.6 x 138.5 cm
Metropolitan Toronto Library, John
Ross Robertson Collection, T-30643

As heretofore, the policy of the school, in accordance with the views of its present Director, is to set the student early at his work for [sic; i.e., from] the life, and to encourage the use of paint and colour from the first.

In answer to criticism of this approach, Eakins replied that he thought the student should learn to draw with colour, "the brush being a more powerful and rapid tool than the point or stump." Further,

> still the main thing that the brush secures is the instant grasp of the grand construction of the figure. There are no lines in nature,...; there are only form and color. The least important, the most changeable, the most difficult thing to catch about a figure is the outline.... The outline is not the man; the grand construction is. Once that is got, the details follow naturally.... The first thing to attend to in painting the model are the movement and the general color. The figure must balance, appear solid and of the right weight. The movement once understood, every detail of the action will be an integral part of the main continuous action; and every detail of color auxiliary to the main system of light and shade. The student should learn to block up his figure rapidly, and then give to any part of it the highest finish without injuring its unity.[13]

The small oil sketches Reid executed at the Pennsylvania Academy in 1883 (nos. 4-6) illustrate the practical application of Eakins's teaching. The unidealized nudes were masked by tradition to protect the models' identities (although the use of a mask was left to the discretion of the model); the American painter Kenyon Cox's pencil drawing *Life Class, Masked Female Nude*, 1876 (fig. 8), is an earlier example. Reid's sketches contain no definite outline; instead, the forms were created by building up layers of colour. Progressively lighter tones were applied over the basic system of light and shadow. The outer contours are uneven, sometimes almost blending into the solid neutral background, and sometimes

Fig. 7
Thomas Eakins
Arcadia 1883
Oil on canvas
98.1 x 114.3 cm
The Metropolitan Museum of Art, New York, Bequest of Miss Adelaide Milton de Groot, 1967

enhanced by a shadow-line used to tidy up the forms (as in the bent right arm of no. 6). Reid applied this technique to the figures in the early *Street Scene, Malaga, Spain*, 1885 (no. 10).[14] This oil was probably painted during the honeymoon trip he made that year with fellow Philadelphia Academy student Mary Hiester, during which they visited Mary Hiester's sister Caroline, a nun in the Malaga convent. There he both etched and painted her portrait (no. 9).

In both this picture and the small *Self Portrait* (no.7) done in Philadelphia (perhaps in the portrait class at the Academy), the layers or blocks of colour used to model the forms have been carefully blended, so that there is a smooth transition from plane to plane and a higher degree of academic finish than was the case in the small oil sketches or *esquisses*. These portraits have that precise quality, based on careful observation and a thorough understanding of anatomy, which also characterizes Eakins's paintings.

Eakins's approach to teaching at the Academy was founded on careful observation of the real world; he was a *réaliste par excellence*. He incorporated lectures on perspective and composition into the curriculum in 1882; a statement to that effect was added to the *Circular* that year, and in 1884 these lectures became a permanent part of the course. His own pictures were often based on complicated perspectival constructions and careful studies (of waves, for instance), which he would apply to works such as *Sailboats Racing on the Delaware*

(1874). Reid's approach, by contrast, was more conceptual;[15] he schematized the wave formations into a series of wavy lines, both in *Toronto Bay* and in *Notre-Dame, Paris*, 1888 (no. 27).

Of great importance was the emphasis Eakins placed on the practice of dissection for advanced students. Eakins believed that "to draw the human figure it is necessary to know as much as possible about it, about its structure and its movements, its bones and muscles, how they are made and how they act."[16] Reid was one of the student demonstrators in anatomy and perspective at the Academy.

Yet another innovation of Eakins was his establishment of a separate modelling class for painters. Although sculpture was not formally taught, modelling in clay and wax was deemed to aid in the painter's grasp of form, helping him or her to avoid losing volume in the painted image. There was interaction, then, between the painters and sculptors; Reid's *Study of a Young Man Done in the Academy of Fine Arts, Philadelphia* (no. 4) is a portrait of Charles Grafly, the sculptor. Eakins, who had studied sculpture in Paris, was very interested in the art of the bas-relief, a subject on which he chose to lecture. None of the small exercises done in the modelling class has been preserved; the sculpting materials were apparently recycled at the end of each class. Reid must have learned the art of bas-relief in Philadelphia - his small relief of *Music*, ca. 1910 (no. 53), demonstrates a good command of a difficult medium, halfway between sculpture and painting, whose effect depends on a subtle interplay of light and shadow.[17]

What impact did Eakins have on Reid, who was his student at the time that the former was most influential at the Pennsylvania Academy? To Eakins the younger painter owed a solid understanding of the human figure, a realistic approach to art based on a close observation of natural phenomena, and the use of models and props for composition - the strongest features, in other words, of the curriculum. His figures have solidity and his compositions evince a sensitive balance between open, loosely painted areas and those executed in greater detail. In the early *Portrait of Mary Hiester Reid*, 1885 (no. 8), highlighted areas display the most attention to detail (the sitter's gloved hands, for instance), as do the zither-player's head and shirt in Eakins's *Professionals at Rehearsal.*

Fig. 8
Kenyon Cox
Life Class, Masked Female Nude
1876
Pencil on cream paper
44.8 x 29.9 cm
The Pennsylvania Academy of the Fine Arts, Purchased with Funds from the H.J. Heinz II Charitable and Family Trust

19

6
Study of a Woman with arms on head done at the Academy of Fine Arts, Philadelphia   1884
Oil on paper
18.6 x 9.5 cm
Art Gallery of Ontario, Gift of Mary Wrinch Reid to the E.P. Taylor Reference Library, 1957, Transferred to the painting collection, 1982

Reid has used a similar palette, consisting of a rich mahogany-like monochrome enlivened by areas of impasto in a lighter hue, which was influenced by Spanish painting, particularly that of Velasquez. It was in Philadelphia that Reid first learned of this master. Eakins, who had visited Spain in 1869, was one of the first American artists to see Spanish art in Spain, when there was little of it available for viewing outside its country of origin, and when he was still of an impressionable age. Lloyd Goodrich, his biographer, lists the qualities that most struck Eakins about Velasquez: his portrayal of real life and real people; his obvious love of character over ideal beauty; a style related to visual reality; his mastery of light and its effects on colour and value; and his austerity, simplification and deliberately reserved colour harmonies.[18] This appreciation for Velasquez was passed on to Reid, who, on his first trip to Europe in 1885, made an unsuccessful attempt to visit Madrid in hopes of seeing the Spanish artist's work with his own eyes. After the Reids finally did get to Madrid in the 1890s, Mary Hiester Reid recorded her and her husband's sustained admiration for Velasquez in a three-part article in *Massey's Magazine*.[19]

Reid benefitted greatly from his training with Eakins at the Pennsylvania Academy, but he was also affected by the weaknesses inherent in the programme. Eakins has been criticized by recent scholars for narrowing the scope of his teaching by placing too much emphasis on working from the nude human figure, and for unduly stressing method over style. Other elements, such as composition and design, were neglected, and his teaching was not effective for students who did not share his particular interests or establish a personal rapport with him - which Reid seems to have enjoyed - since these other interests were not encouraged.[20]

For instance, while Eakins to advised his students to "'Get the portrait of the light, the kind of day it is, if it is cold or warm, gray or sunny, and what time of day it is...,'"[21] Maria Chamberlin-Hellman, author of a thesis on Eakins as a teacher, has observed that he did not lecture on theories of light and colour. He left his students on their own "to grapple with the complicated problems of the effects of natural light and atmosphere on colour," for which practice Chamberlin-Hellman offers the possible explanation that the painting lessons learned from direct observation of optical phenomena, without the interposition of instruments or theories, were difficult, if not impossible, to reconcile with the entire framework of academic method espoused by Eakins as a student and teacher. Eakins, by nature and education, was distrustful of purely subjective approaches to painting. Consequently, consideration of this material of import to painting students of the 1870s and 1880s was limited in Eakins' classes at the Pennsylvania Academy.[22]

Reid captured the strong warm light of southern Spain in *Street Scene, Malaga, Spain,* and no less effectively used the clear summer light of his native southwestern Ontario to render the sculptural quality of the foreground figure in *The Call to Dinner,* 1886-87 (no. 12), his first large-scale genre picture. However, like the nude studies done at the Academy, the figures in the street scene have been placed against a neutral wall in a shallow space with a strong theatrical light directed on them. This casts a shadow to the left of the figures, with the result that they stand out in relief.

In *The Call to Dinner,* the figure of Susan, Reid's sister, stands out, again like a figure in relief, before what amounts to a backdrop, for she is not effectively connected to the landscape before her.[23] This lack of integration between figure and setting was most obvious in Reid's outdoor scenes, though he was not unfamiliar with the painting of landscapes. A good part of his early output consisted of landscape or view paintings, and he had participated in Eakins's outdoor sketching classes. Major paintings like *In the Gloaming,* 1883 (painted in Philadelphia), *The Last Load,* first exhibited in 1884, *'Twixt Night and Day, On the Grand Canal, Venice,* both shown in the 1886 OSA annual exhibition (fig. 9), and *Toronto Bay,* 1887, indicate that landscape formed a major part of his oeuvre. He ran into problems, however, when it came to incorporating figures into these compositions. The staffage figures in *Notre-Dame,* for instance, seem to have been added as an afterthought, for the pen-and-ink sketch (no. 26) contains no figures. For interiors, Reid often fell back on the use of a window as the main source of directed light to unify the composition. *At the Window,* 1888 (no. 13), is an example in which the disjunction between figure and landscape is permissible

No. 64 —On the Grand Canal, Venice.—G. A. Reid.

Fig. 9
George A. Reid
On the Grand Canal, Venice 1886
Pen-and-ink rendering after the painting, reproduced in the catalogue of the 14th Annual Exhibition of the Ontario Society of Artists, 1886, p. 22

because of their physical separation by the wall and window. The reason for this lack of integration lies in the fact that while the landscape was probably done *in situ*, the figural elements, like Susan in *The Call to Dinner*, were done indoors in a studio setting with appropriate props under theatrical lighting.

Paris

George Reid's taste for the Parisian painting to which he had been introduced by Harris and Eakins was whetted by the six-month trip to Europe he made in 1885 with his new bride. In Paris they visited the Luxembourg Museum, the major repository of contemporary French painting (now the Musée d'Orsay), whose collection was built up through purchases from the annual Salons. Here they were especially impressed by the work of Gérôme, Alexandre Cabanel, Manet, Bastien-Lepage, Tony Robert-Fleury, Courbet, Renoir, and Luc-Olivier Merson.[24] These for the most part were "*juste-milieu*" painters, or ones who followed a "middle-of-the-road" aesthetic, and reflected the worldwide shift from a classic-romantic to a realist mode and from a linear to a painterly treatment.[25]

This trip was too brief, however, and the Reids had to wait until 1888 before they could return to Paris. This second visit was financed by an exhibition and sale at Oliver, Coate and Co., of 17 King Street East, Toronto, in late May of 1888. One hundred and thirty works by both George and Mary Hiester Reid, reflecting their output of the previous three years, were on view. The sale was extremely successful, judging from the list of purchasers recorded in Reid's copy of the catalogue,[26] and from the praise he received in the press. A contemporary critic observed,

The main characteristics of Mr. Reid's work are boldness and truth, a

27
Notre-Dame, Paris 1888
Oil on panel
22.9 x 33.9 cm
Art Gallery of Ontario, Purchased
with funds made available from the
Estate of Margaret L. Thomas,
Toronto, 1984

thorough acquaintance with anatomy, the laws of perspective, and rules of composition, a great facility of execution and breadth of treatment.[27]

Perhaps the reviewer derived these remarks from an interview with Reid, in which the artist emphasized Eakins-like principles that would still have been immediate to him. The couple departed for the continent soon after.

Like most other North American student-artists in Paris, Reid enrolled at the Académie Julian, the most popular of the "ateliers" that offered an alternative to the Ecole des Beaux-Arts. The English painter William Rothenstein, who attended Julian's around the same time as did Reid, described it as a

> congeries of studios crowded with students, the walls thick with palette scrapings, hot, airless and extremely noisy....
> Julian himself knew nothing of the arts.... He had persuaded a number of well-known painters and sculptors to act as visiting professors....[28]

Among these visitors were Bouguereau, Jules Lefebvre, Benjamin Constant and Lucien Doucet. As Rothenstein recalled,

> To find a place among the closely-packed easels and tabourets was not easy. It seemed that wherever one settled one was in somebody's way.... [T]he variety of drawing and painting at Julian's was highly stimulating. Puvis de Chavannes and Monet were the most prevalent influences among the more intelligent students; but the Salon conventions were still active, and especially affected the painting of the nude.[29]

Reid studied with Constant (on the advice of fellow Canadian Paul Peel, who had been living in Paris since 1882) at the Académie Julian. His life studies done there reflect the conditions described by Rothenstein, which explains the peculiar angles from which the models were viewed and painted (nos. 14-17). This is apparent in the nude he did (known today only from a photograph; see fig. 10) for the annual competition or *Concours* at the Julian in 1889, in which five hundred students worked from the model for one week. Reid won a silver medal for this entry. In addition, Reid's nudes display the conventional academic finish - the conservative approach on which Rothenstein had commented.

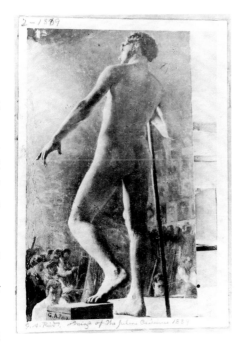

Fig. 10
George A. Reid, Entry for the 1889 *Concours* that won a prize at the Académie Julian, Paris. Present whereabouts unknown; reproduced from a contemporary photograph in George Reid Scrapbook, vol. 1, E.P. Taylor Reference Library, Art Gallery of Ontario.

However, his work was received favourably by Constant, who commented on "*le joli ton*" of one of his figures (perhaps no. 18), saying it was like a Rubens in the Louvre, which he encouraged Reid to go and see.[30]

While mornings were spent at Julian's, Reid went to the Académie Colarossi three afternoons and evenings a week for costume and life classes (no. 19). He also studied composition at the Colarossi, supplementing similar studies at the Julian to make up for his weak training in this area. *Composition, Julian Academy* (Hannibal crossing the Alps) (no. 22), which Constant had suggested he work up into a large salon painting, *Job* (no. 20), and *The Sword of Damocles, Julian Academy* (no. 21) are three compositional sketches or *esquisses*.

These sketches were an integral part of the academic approach. In them, the artist would work out his composition, the major movements and directions, and the areas of tonal contrast. The unified relation of light and dark values resulted in "*l'effet,*" the successful combination of disparate elements by means of light. In both *Job* and *The Sword of Damocles, Julian Academy* a sidelight falls across the figures, uniting the scene. The surfaces are loosely painted in unmixed colours; the lack of blended middle tones resulted in a greater contrast in values than one would find in the large finished work. The sketches would be painted for their own sake or as stock images for possible incorporation into a larger picture at a later date. Examples are the sketches executed at the Cluny Museum (nos. 23-25), or those done elsewhere in and around Paris (no. 33).

While Reid was used to making pen-and-ink sketches, having learned the medium from W.A. Langton in Toronto, he does not seem to have adopted the practice of making studies in oil until he went to Paris. There he continued to make ink sketches, some of which, like *Notre-Dame, Paris* (no. 26), were made on location as accurate renderings of an observed scene for a larger painting. In this particular case, Reid may have worked from another sketch, since some visible alterations have been made to the finished painting: the view is from further west along the banks of the Seine, so that the Pont de l'Archéveché is no longer in the foreground, and the length of the nave visible between the south transept and south tower is greater.

For *Logging* (no. 32), the first sketch and second study (no. 30, A and B) were done in oil; at this initial stage, the basic format and disposition of figures were established, followed by a number of *études* or detailed studies in pen-and-ink (nos. 28 and 29). Reid painted a more finished *étude* in oil (no. 31) of one of the loggers, which was dropped unaltered into the large canvas. The preliminary sketches were made in a timber yard in the fall of 1888 near Reid's studio at 65 Boulevard Arago, where, upon discovering the location with "great logs resembling those found in Canada," he "seized the opportunity to paint a Canadian picture."[31] The full-scale canvas, which was sent to the annual exhibitions of the Ontario Society of Artists and the Art Association of Montreal in 1889, was preceded by a smaller study which was not completed until 1931.

The importance of the sketch cannot be overestimated. It played an especially significant role in the later nineteenth century, when emphasis shifted from the highly finished final product to the preparatory stages of painting.[32] The sketch was valued because it embodied both the expression of an original idea, and the individual sensibility of the artist through the spontaneity and freedom visible in the brushwork. Gradually, sketch-like qualities were retained in the finished work. The academic practice of making these preparatory sketches allowed the student more freedom to manoeuvre within the system. Albert Boime, a scholar of nineteenth-century academic art, has concluded that the academy system contributed to the evolution of independent tendencies because "the qualities eventually associated with the aesthetics of the sketch were exactly those which had been assigned to the preparatory sketch throughout the history of the Academy; the independents had only to shift emphasis from the executive to the generative phase and systematize the sketching procedures."[33]

Upon his return to Toronto in the fall of 1889, George Reid began producing large-scale genre pictures, after fitting up his new studio in the Yonge Street Arcade into settings for his paintings: a hayloft, a parlour, and a council room. Four studies for major paintings executed over the next few years are included in this exhibition: sketches for *The Story*, 1890 (no. 35), *Mortgaging the Homestead*, 1890 (no. 38), *Family*

37
The Other Side of the Question   1890
Oil on canvas
104.0 x 132.5 cm
Art Gallery of Ontario, Purchase,
1985

Fig. 11
George A. Reid working on *The Fore-closure of the Mortgage*, 1893. Photo Services Department, Art Gallery of Ontario.

Prayer, 1890 (no. 41), and *The Foreclosure of the Mortgage*, 1893 (no. 46). Like his composition studies done at the Académie Julian, these sketches were used by Reid to establish the major figural groupings and their psychological reactions to the main action. These reactions were emphasized by the fall of light on the figures.

For *The Story* (no. 36), it is likely that Reid painted the sketch rapidly, then paid some young boys to come to the studio to pose for him. He always worked from specific props and models and went to great lengths to make his settings believable. In *The Other Side of the Question* (no. 37), the central seated figure at the far side of the table resembles Adam Reid, the artist's father (see no. 11), and the very elderly man to the left of the picture may have been Joseph Shuter, who had been the subject of an earlier Reid canvas, *The Flute Player*, in 1886. The contemporary map of Canada and the print of Queen Victoria on the wall signal this as being a Canadian picture.

The sketch could also serve as a record of a painting that Reid was sending to an exhibition, or which had already been sold. *Family Prayer*, 1890 (no. 40), was first exhibited in the 1891 annual exhibitions of the

Royal Canadian Academy and the Art Association of Montreal, then at the Pennsylvania Academy, and finally the Paris Salon in 1892. The large canvas bears the date 1890; the sketch, 1892.[34] The sketch contains elements lacking in the canvas, such as the table leg behind the child kneeling to the left of the mother in the central group, and an article of clothing, both of which were painted out, probably at a later date. This study may have been done to replace an earlier sketch, now lost, or, more likely, as a record of the work to show to prospective buyers when the artist knew the painting would be out of the studio, particularly when it travelled to Paris in 1892.

While the sketches have a loose, impressionistic quality, little of this was transferred to the paintings. The compositions adhere to the standard academic norm, stable circular and triangular groupings dominating. In both *Forbidden Fruit* (no. 34) and *The Story*, completed just after Reid's return to Toronto, the figures are solidly constructed, their forms built up by smoothly blended layers of colour. A contemporary American artist and reviewer, Charles Henry Hart, commented on *Forbidden Fruit*'s academic qualities, writing, "It is well drawn and nice in tone."[35] A looser, more impressionistic approach was confined to the treatment of the hay.

What effect did Reid's experience in Paris have on his painting? Was he able to incorporate elements of the new Impressionism into his own work as the "*juste milieu*" painters had done? By 1893, the year of the World's Columbian Exposition in Chicago, the French influence was all-pervasive in the United States; this was noted by William A. Sherwood (1859-1919), another former student of the Pennsylvania Academy, in a review of the art department of the World's Columbian Exposition, Chicago, that appeared in *Canadian Magazine*.[36] Even in 1890, Charles Henry Hart, writing about the Pennsylvania Academy exhibition in which Reid participated, had remarked that "No sooner has the school of realism gone out of fashion than the school of impressionism comes in; and, strange to say, these two diverse schools are often spoken of as if they were synonymous instead of being as far apart as are the antipodes...."[37]

What Reid gained from his Parisian experience was primarily a more unified picture, and a better understanding of *l'effet*, that is, an atmosphere unified by a softly diffused light. In both his indoor and outdoor scenes, there is an absence of the harsh outlines of his earlier work. Now forms are more generalized, or "softened" by an underpainting ("*l'ébauche*") - a terra-cotta colour, for instance, in *The Other Side of the Question*, or a grey-blue one in *The Berry Pickers* (no. 42), which are permitted to show through in certain areas, and over which the highlights are loosely brushed to model the forms - as in the eldest man's hands in *The Other Side of the Question*.

The figures in *The Berry Pickers*, in contrast to that of the woman in *The Call to Dinner*, are better integrated into their landscape setting, probably as a result of this underpainting and the overall softer focus that results. Lucius O'Brien, first president of the Royal Canadian Academy, was to criticize artists using this style, calling them "The Eliminators," and feared that they would bring about the ruin of easel-painting in this country because of their neglect of detail. Reid's biographer Muriel Miller (Miner) explained this change in Reid's style as a possible result of his new interest in mural painting, which dates from his Paris sojourn of 1888, mural painting being a medium that necessitates the generalizing of forms in order for them to be easily "read" from a distance. Reid began studying mural painting around 1889, inspired by the example of Puvis de Chavannes and the murals being done in the Hôtel de Ville in Paris. While a more even internal lighting was required in murals, this does not, however, fully explain the more unified effect evident in this work, which was learned in the Paris ateliers.

A contemporary article spoke of *The Berry Pickers* as a most characteristic work of George Reid, showing "his skill in composition, his capable and comprehensive drawing and his truthful rendering of sunlight effects."[38] The technique of the painting is a watered-down version of Impressionism, but Reid would get closer to full Impressionism later in the 1890s. The small sketch of *Mrs. Parker, Onteora*, 1892 (no. 44), for instance, being a sketch and therefore much more loosely handled, is a fully Impressionist work.

**54
Study for Decorative Panel, Music
1900
Pastel on cardboard
40.3 x 14.5 cm
Art Gallery of Ontario, Gift of Mary
Wrinch Reid, 1954

Sympathetic Realism:
Paintings for the Salon

The years 1890-1893 were particularly busy ones for Reid. He painted major canvases and sent them to all the important exhibitions in both Canada and the United States, often winning prizes for his entries (no. 1). *The Foreclosure of the Mortgage* (no. 47) won him a bronze medal at the World's Columbian Exposition in 1893, and another at the California Mid-winter International Exposition, San Francisco, in 1894. *Music*, 1900 (no. 56), won him a bronze medal at the St. Louis Universal Exposition in 1904. He sent work to the Paris Salon in 1889 (*Dreaming* and *Autumn*), 1890 (*The Story*), 1891 (*The Berry Pickers*), 1892 (*Lullaby*), 1893 (*A Modern Madonna*), and 1896 (*Portrait*).

In 1890 Reid painted two major canvases: *The Other Side of the Question*, whose completion was marked by a private view at his studio on 12 April 1890, and *Mortgaging the Homestead* (no. 39), which was his RCA Diploma Work, deposited that year, in conjunction with his becoming a full Academician. Both paintings were described as being " realistic presentiment[s] of the Life around us," where there is "no straining after meretricious effect." Instead, "they are just simple, strong, natural and masterly...."[39]

It was Reid's self-expressed intention to "represent possible episodes in life" as realistically as he was able, "by means of the best technique" at his command.[40] He focused on the common man, and for this reason was compared to the contemporary French painter Jules Breton (1827-1906), who specialized in French peasant subjects.[41] Reid insisted that he was not suggesting any theory of social or economic reform, although it was his wish to "direct attention to mortgages, which are engulfing millions of homes intended to be the joy and hope of their founders."[42] The immediate inspiration for *Mortgaging the Homestead* was his learning of the plight of Dakota farmers, but the canvas also harkened back to his own childhood experience, as did many of his pictures of this period, such as *Forbidden Fruit*. These scenes were meant to have

Fig. 12
Thomas Hovenden
Breaking Home Ties   1890
Oil on canvas
132.4 x 183.5 cm
Philadelphia Museum of Art: Given
by Ellen Harrison McMichael in
memory of C. Emory McMichael

a direct appeal to the viewer, and while they may not have been intended to expound any political views, they were heavily moralistic. There is little physical activity in them; rather, the action is on an emotional and psychological level. The viewer is drawn in and manipulated not only through compositional devices, such as an open foreground or the outward glance of the young mother in *Mortgaging the Homestead*, but by the emotional pull created by the expressions and attitudes of the figures.

Of *Mortgaging the Homestead* and *The Foreclosure of the Mortgage* (not to be regarded as its sequel), Reid wrote,

When the artist sees that our vaunted progress not only suffers no adequate relief, but seems to aggrevate sorrow and suffering, he must express himself for the sake of his devotion to the beautiful, for his love of truth, for his desire that life should be made to develop all its noblest possibilities, nor without motive or appeal to result. I thoroughly agree with the view that demands the best possible expression of an idea. Then when the artist is true to himself, his work must exhibit the purpose for which he has striven, and in proportion as his character is noble and enlightened, will he create works possessing these qualities.

A middle position, then, demands that the idea and expression be adequate to each other.[43]

The concept of the union of expression and idea, mentioned in the passage quoted above, was one of the qualities the Reids found and admired in Velasquez on their second extended European sojourn in 1896. In Mary Hiester Reid's words,

The combination of freedom of handling with perfect tone and beauty of handling have never been equalled.... His painting is robust, with no affectations; realistic, yet with infinite delicacy of modelling.... There is not... that separation of the method of expression from the idea to be expressed.[44]

It was on this trip that Reid painted his copy of the Velasquez *Portrait of a Dwarf with a Dog* (no. 49).

Reid's large salon paintings or "machines" from the 1890s were very popular, particularly *The Foreclosure of the Mortgage*[45] (fig. 11), of 1893, which, apart from winning prizes, received several glowing reviews when it was shown in Chicago. The *New York Times*, for instance, declared that "The artist's control of the light and utilizing of the figures to contribute to the general effect are masterly. The painting makes a vivid impression." The *New York American*'s reviewer wrote that "The poses and expression of face of each figure is masterful. There is none of the exaggerated sadness which repels, so often seen in pictures dealing with such subjects."[46]

At the Chicago Exposition in 1893 the American genre painter Thomas Hovenden (1840-1895) showed his *Breaking Home Ties* (fig. 12), the theme of which was similar to that of Reid's *Mortgaging the Homestead* and *The Foreclosure of the Mortgage*: the tenuous nature of farm life. In Hovenden's picture, the young man is obliged to leave home and seek work elsewhere. Indeed, Reid continued to share much in common with his American contemporaries, treating many of the same subjects, which were equally popular in the European salons. The mother-and-child theme, for instance (nos. 48 and 51), was done many times by Reid: two large examples, *Lullaby*, 1892, and *A Modern Madonna*, 1893, were both hung in the Paris Salon, attesting to their popularity with contemporary international audiences. Scenes involving children were also favoured: Reid's *The Visit to the Clock-cleaner*, 1893, was painted the same year as Hovenden's *Travelling Clockmaker*.[47] Both show children captivated by the old men's craft.

Apart from their obvious human appeal, Reid saw these subjects as "new world subject matter," and he is quoted as saying:

> So far...Canadian artists have been chiefly influenced by the French and English schools, but [he] feels...that the Canadian brush is bound to have for its ultimate end the expression of Canadian life, sentiments and characteristics; the expression in short, by genre pictures, and by symbolic and historical conceptions of the idea of nationality, and the development of a country so vast as ours.[48]

As it turned out, Canadian nationalism, which began to grow in the 1890s, ultimately found its expression in landscape rather than in genre painting early in the twentieth century. Reid himself later turned more seriously to landscape painting, although he had painted landscapes throughout his career. He held fast, however, to the use of the figure, the allegorical figure being an integral part of many of his murals (no. 57).

Conclusion

After their visit to Spain in 1896, the Reids stopped on their way home for a couple of months in Paris, where he studied at the Julian Académie, and she at the Colarossi. Their intention was to brush up on their painting and "get first hand acquaintance with the new Impressionistic method of painting."[49] In Paris, Reid carried on painting academic nudes (no. 50), and continued to do so after his return to Canada. *Seated Nude Study* (no. 52) was painted in the Royal Canadian Academy Life Class in 1898. The later *Portrait, Mary Hiester*, 1898 (no. 51), demonstrates a more complete application of impressionistic techniques and stands in marked contrast to the earlier, more formal version done in 1885 (no. 8).

The academic training George Reid received in Toronto, Philadelphia and Paris, which he had applied with great success to his large genre pictures, was in turn put to use in his mural painting. Mural projects increasingly took over his time, beginning in the mid-1890s.[50] He saw the mural as a more effective means of visual communication than genre compositions and landscapes, because it was fully integrated into its setting and allowed for grander subjects, such as episodes from Canadian history. The decorative panel *Music*, 1900 (no. 56), was meant to form the right-hand panel of a triptych (no. 55) - a popular format of the day, to be placed within an architectural setting. A small relief and a pastel study (nos. 53 and 54) for *Music* are also included in this exhibition.

Once mural painting captured Reid's interest, his production of genre pictures for the salon dropped off. Similar themes bracket the years 1880 to around 1895: nude studies (intended only as studies, never as subjects in and of themselves), portraits (of himself and his wife, as illustrated here), and his copies (after Robert Harris and Velasquez). The human figure is central to his approach, which remained essentially academic. Around 1892, the figures were gradually removed from a realist context within the easel painting and entered the more abstract realm of allegory in his decorative murals.

It was in his contributions to the art of mural painting that Reid proved to be most influential. A number of his private pupils, and several of his students at the Ontario College of Art, whose first principal he became in 1912, and from which he retired in 1929, went on to establish reputations for themselves as prominent muralists - most notably, F.S. Challener and C.W. Jefferys. Although his own painting style became looser and more impressionistic in the 1910s and '20s, as a teacher George Reid never abandoned his loyalty to "the great academic tradition."

Endnotes

1 Hjalmar Hjorth Boyesen, "Boyhood and Girlhood," *The Monthly Illustrator* 4 (April 1895): 6-7. Boyesen wrote: "With that sympathetic realism which has characterized his pictures of more adult persons and more serious scenes, he has given us here the boy and the girl which we know, and which we were, and it does us good to have those days so recalled. Like so many other contemporary painters, Reid was depicting an idealized past, drawing on his own personal experiences."

2 Stanley G. Moyer, "Interpreting the Pioneers: A Study of the Dean of Canadian Artists, George Agnew Reid...," *The Canadian Magazine* 76 (August 1931): 17-18, 36.

3 H. Barbara Weinberg, "The Lure of Paris: Late-Nineteenth-Century American Painters and their French Training," in *A* New World: Masterpieces of American Painting 1760-1910 (Boston: The Museum of Fine Arts Boston, 1983), p. 30.

4 Albert Boime, *Thomas Couture and the Eclectic Vision* (New Haven: Yale University Press, 1980), p. 457.

5 For a history of the academy tradition, see Albert Boime, The Academy and French Painting in the Nineteenth Century (London: Phaidon Publishers, 1971).

6 Muriel Miller Miner, *G.A. Reid: Canadian Artist* (Toronto: The Ryerson Press, 1946), p. 24.

7 Ibid., p. 19.

8 G.A. Reid, quoted by Moncrieff Williamson in *Island Painter: The Life of Robert Harris (1849-1919)* (Charlottetown: Ragweed Press, 1983), pp. 70-71.

9 In a letter dated 22 November 1939 to the Babcock Galleries, New York, Reid wrote expressing an interest in Eakins and requesting a copy of the catalogue of the Eakins exhibition that he had heard was being held there. Philadelphia Museum of Art files, *Professionals at Rehearsal*, S-52.

10 Miner, *G.A. Reid*, p. 12.

11 William C. Brownell, "The Art Schools of Philadelphia," *Scribner's Monthly: An Illustrated Magazine for the People* 18 (September 1879): 737-50.

12 Reid to E.C. Babcock, 4 December 1939, from the Collection of Lloyd Goodrich, quoted in part in Maria Chamberlin-Hellman, "Thomas Eakins as a

Teacher," unpublished Doctoral thesis for Columbia University, 1981, pp. 194-95, note 206.

13 Brownell, "The Art Schools of Philadelphia": 740-41.

14 This painting just recently resurfaced. On the basis of style and subject matter, the writer has presumed it to be *Street Scene, Malaga*, which was exhibited in Reid's 1888 sale at Oliver, Coate and Co., Toronto.

15 For a comparison of Reid and Eakins, see Ann Davis, "Seekers After Reality: Thomas Eakins and George Reid," in *A Distant Harmony: Comparisons in the Painting of Canada and the United States of America* (Winnipeg: The Winnipeg Art Gallery, 1982), pp. 71-101.

16 Brownell, "The Art Schools of Philadelphia": 745.

17 Reid exhibited a number of sculpted works: for example, *Study of a Figure* and *The Zither Player*, in the 1884 OSA annual exhibition, and a bas-relief in the 1903 OSA.

18 Lloyd Goodrich, *Thomas Eakins* (Cambridge, Massachusetts and London: Harvard University Press, published for the National Gallery of Art, Washington, 1982), vol. 1, pp. 59-60.

19 By that time, however, there were other qualities in Velasquez' paintings that the Reids appreciated: see note 44.

20 Louise Lippincott, "Thomas Eakins and the Academy," in *In this Academy: The Pennsylvania Academy of the Fine Arts 1805-1976* (Philadelphia: Pennsylvania Academy of the Fine Arts, 1976), p. 177. See also Elizabeth Johns, "Thomas Eakins and 'Pure Art Education'," *Archives of American Art Journal* 23 (1983): 2-5.

21 Quoted by Charles Bregler in "Thomas Eakins as a Teacher," *The Arts* 17 (March 1931), and excerpted in Goodrich, *Thomas Eakins*, vol. 1, p. 185.

22 Chamberlin-Hellman, "Thomas Eakins as a Teacher," pp. 293-94.

23 Ann Davis has made this same observation in "Seekers after Reality: Thomas Eakins and George Reid," in *A Distant Harmony*, p. 95.

24 Miner, *G.A. Reid*, p. 32.

25 Boime, *Thomas Couture*, p. 558.

26 George Reid Scrapbook, vol. 1, pp. 116-127. The scrapbook is housed in the E.P. Taylor Reference Library, Art Gallery of Ontario.

27 "Art and Artists," *The Mail and Empire* (Toronto), undated clipping in George Reid Scrapbook, vol. 1, p. 116.

28 William Rothenstein, *Men and Memories: A History of the Arts 1872-1922* (New York: Tudor Publishing, 1951), 2 vols. in 1, pp. 36, 39.

29 *Ibid.*, pp. 37, 43.

30 Miner, *G.A. Reid*, p. 51.

31 G.A. Reid, artist's typewritten statement to accompany the picture *Logging*, dated 7 October 1941, in George Reid scrapbook, vol. 1, p. 132.

32 Boime, *The Academy and French Painting in the Nineteenth Century*, p. 86.

33 *Ibid.*, p. 185.

34 The vague inscription, when examined under a magnifying glass, appears to read "1892."

35 Charles Henry Hart, "The Pennsylvania Academy Exhibition," in *The Independent* (Philadelphia), 13 March 1890. I am grateful to Jeannette Tookey for finding this reference for me.

36 *The Canadian Magazine* 1: 638-41.

37 Hart, "The Pennsylvania Academy Exhibition."

38 "George Agnew Reid, R.C.A.," unsourced clipping, possibly a prospectus for a book titled *Masterpieces of Modern Painting* (never published?), in George Reid Scrapbook, vol. 1, p. 156.

39 "Canadian Art. Mr. G.A. Reid Paints Two More Life-like Pictures," unsourced (Toronto?) newspaper clipping dated 15 April 1890, in George Reid Scrapbook, vol. 1, p. 150.

40 George A. Reid, "The Evolution of Two of my Pictures," *Massey's Magazine* 1(January 1896): 14; in George Reid Scrapbook, vol. 1, p. 155.

41 Matthews Brothers and Co., Toronto, *Work Executed During the Summer of 1890 by G.A. Reid, R.C.A.* (Toronto: Matthews Bros. and Co., 1890), in George Reid Scrapbook, vol. 1, p. 155.

42 George Reid, "The Evolution of Two of My Pictures": 14; in George Reid Scrapbook, vol. 1, p. 155.

43 *Ibid*: 14.

44 Mary Hiester Reid, "From Gibraltar to the Pyrenees," *Massey's Magazine* 2 (May 1896): 384.

45 The painting won a medal both in Chicago in 1893 and in San Francisco in 1894. In 1919, having been shown at the 1913 Royal Academy exhibition, it was burned in a warehouse fire in London. Reid repainted it in 1934, and it is this second version that is in the Government of Ontario Art Collection, Ontario Legislative Building, Queen's Park, Toronto.

46 Clippings in George Reid Scrapbook, vol. 1, p 319.

47 A pen-and-ink drawing after Reid's painting is reproduced in Miner, *G.A. Reid*, p. 65; the Hovenden appeared on the cover of the *Kennedy Quarterly* 3 (April 1962).

48 "A Canadian Artist," *Home Magazine* (21 May 1908): 906; in George Reid Scrapbook, vol. 1, p. 280.

49 Miner, *G.A. Reid*, p. 88.

50 See Rosalind Pepall, "The Murals by George A. Reid in the Toronto Municipal Buildings (1897-1899)," MA thesis, Concordia University, 1982.

Bibliography

Boime, Albert. *The Academy and French Painting in the Nineteenth Century.* London: Phaidon Publishers, 1971.

Boime, Albert. *Thomas Couture and the Eclectic Vision.* New Haven: Yale University Press, 1980.

Boyesen, Hjalmar Hjorth. "Boyhood and Girlhood." *The Monthly Illustrator* 4 (April 1895): 2-8.

Brownell, William C. "The Art Schools of Philadelphia." *Scribner's Monthly: An Illustrated Magazine for the People* 18 (September 1879): 737-50.

Chamberlin-Hellman, Maria. "Thomas Eakins as a Teacher." Unpublished Doctoral thesis for Columbia University, 1981.

Davis, Ann. *A Distant Harmony: Comparisons in the Painting of Canada and the United States of America.* Winnipeg: The Winnipeg Art Gallery, 1982.

Dickman, Chris. *G.A. Reid: Towards a Union of the Arts.* Durham, Ontario: Durham Art Gallery, 1985.

Fairbairn, Margaret L. "The Art of George Reid." *The Canadian Magazine* 22 (November 1903): 2-9.

The George A. Reid Memorial Exhibition. Catalogue of exhibition held at Art Gallery of Toronto, 6-28 March 1948. Toronto: Art Gallery of Toronto, 1948.

Goodrich, Lloyd. *Thomas Eakins.* Cambridge, Massachusetts and London: Harvard University Press, published for the National Gallery of Art, Washington, vols. 1 and 2, 1982.

Hart, Charles Henry. "The Pennsylvania Academy Exhibition." *The Independent* (Philadelphia), 13 March 1890.

Lippincott, Louise. "Thomas Eakins and the Academy." In *In this Academy: Pennsylvania Academy of the Fine Arts 1805-1976: A Special Bicentennial Exhibition.* Philadelphia: Pennsylvania Academy of the Fine Arts, 1976, pp. 162-87.

Miner, Muriel Miller. *G.A. Reid: Canadian Artist.* Toronto: The Ryerson Press, 1946.

Moyer, Stanley G. "Interpreting the Pioneers: A Study of the Dean of Canadian Artists, George Agnew Reid, R.C.A., O.S.A., Who Has Been So Large a Factor in the Development of Art in Canada." *The Canadian Magazine* 76 (August 1931): 17-18, 36-37.

Reid, George A. *Art Education in the United States, Great Britain, France, Belgium and Holland. A Report to the Council of the Ontario College of Art by the Principal G.A. Reid, R.C.A.* Toronto: Ontario College of Art, 1924?

_____. "The Evolution of Two of my Pictures." *Massey's Magazine* 1 (January 1896): 10-15.

_____. Scrapbooks (c. 1880s-c. 1947) in two volumes, compiled by George A. Reid and housed in the E.P. Taylor Reference Library, Art Gallery of Ontario. Gift of Mrs. G.A. Reid, 1957. Contents of vol. 1 include photographs, memorabilia, and correspondence; reproductions, journal extracts, and clippings; sketches in various media; annotated exhibition catalogues, etc. Contents of vol. 2 include sketches, plans, photographs and clippings dealing with architecture and furniture designs by Reid. Original artworks in vol. 1 were removed and transferred to the Canadian Historical Collection. Both volumes available for consultation on microfiche.

Reid, Mary Hiester. "From Gibraltar to the Pyrenees." Illustrated by G.A. Reid. *Massey's Magazine* 2 (May 1896): 297-308; in George Reid Scrapbook, p. 205.

_____. "From Gibraltar to the Pyrenees. Second Paper." Illustrated by G.A. Reid. *Massey's Magazine* 2 (June 1896): 373-384; in George Reid Scrapbook, p. 206.

_____. "In Northern Spain." Illustrated by G.A. Reid. *Massey's Magazine* 3 (June 1897): 375-383; in George Reid Scrapbook, p. 207.

Rothenstein, William. *Men and Memories: A History of the Arts 1872-1922.* New York: Tudor Publishing, 1951.

Sellin, David. *The First Pose. 1876: Turning Point in American Art. Howard Roberts, Thomas Eakins and A Century of Philadelphia Nudes.* New York: W.W. Norton, Inc., 1976.

Sherwood, William A. "The Influence of the French School upon Recent Art." *The Canadian Magazine* 1 (1893): 638-41.

Walker, Doreen E. "'L'Art pour la Vie': l'esthétique de George Agnew Reid." *Revue de l'Université de Moncton* 15 (Avril-décembre 1982): 49-67.

Weinburg, H. Barbara. *The American Pupils of Jean-Léon Gérôme*. Forth Worth, Texas: Amon Carter Museum, 1984.

_____. "The Lure of Paris: Late-Nineteenth Century American Painters and their French Training." In *A New World: Masterpieces of American Painting 1760-1910*. Boston: The Museum of Fine Arts, 1983, pp. 16-32.

Weisburg, Gabriel. *The Realist Tradition: French Painting and Drawing 1830-1900*. Cleveland: The Cleveland Museum of Art in cooperation with Indiana University Press, c. 1980.

Wunderlich, Rudolf. "Thomas Hovenden and the American Genre Painters." *The Kennedy Quarterly* (New York) 3 (April 1962): 1-48.

Chronology

by Robert Stacey

1860   25 July: born at Wingham, Ontario, son of Adam Reid and Elizabeth Agnew (third of nine children)

1876   Meets Seaforth, Ontario painter William Nichol Cresswell, decides to learn oil painting

1878   Apprenticed to J.B. Proctor, local architect; Fall: to Toronto, where he attends night classes run by Ontario Society of Artists, 14 King St. W.; works as machinist in Toronto Foundry

1879   January-April: attends art classes three nights a week at Ontario School of Art, Toronto; sees annual spring exhibition of OSA; Robert Harris returns from Paris where he had been studying, takes over antique class at Ontario School of Art, introduces "French way of working," thereby changing teaching methods of the school; Reid takes classes in charcoal sketching and oil painting

1880   Wins second place for time sketching and Ontario School of Art President's silver medal for drawing from the antique for *Jason and the Golden Fleece* (done by the Harris method); returns to Wingham to concentrate on portrait painting

1881   Reid first exhibits with OSA, *Still Life, Fruit*

1882   March: Reid returns to Ontario School of Art after 22 months of work as portrait painter in Wingham and Kincardine; exhibits *The Last Load* and *The Chorister* at OSA; October: enrolls in Pennsylvania Academy of the Fine Arts, Philadelphia (to 1885); December: admitted to "night antique class" conducted by Thomas Eakins

1883-84   January-March, October 1883-March 1884: attends Pennsylvania Academy, with full student privileges; serves as an anatomy "demonstrator" under Eakins, 1883-84; April: finishes studies at Pennsylvania Academy

1884   *The Last Load* exhibited at the Pennsylvania Academy

1885   Founder-member, Association of Canadian Etchers; exhibits for first time at Royal Canadian Academy; May: marries fellow student Mary Hiester, then embarks on honeymoon trip abroad to Manchester, London, Paris, Spain, Italy, returning in September; takes quarters at

Adelaide and Toronto Streets, where he opens a studio which he offers to RCA evening life class; elected Associate, RCA

1886   Elected member of OSA; conducts private day and evening art class according to Eakins's teaching methods; moves to new quarters at 31 King St., Toronto; begins *The Call to Dinner*, his first large genre picture; wins bronze medal at Colonial and Indian Exhibition, London

1887   Reid's private life class includes W.W. Alexander, William Bland, F.S. Challener, George Coleman, Alfred Francis, C.W. Jefferys, James Laughlin, Owen Staples, A.H. Hider, and James Langford

1888   Decides to continue art studies abroad, so transfers private students to Toronto Art Students' League (founded 1886); May 28-30: *Exhibition of Paintings by Mr. and Mrs. George Agnew Reid* at Oliver, Coate and Co., Toronto; June: to Paris with M.H. Reid, meets fellow Canadian artist Paul Peel (in Paris since 1882), studies at Julian and Colarossi academies until October 1889

1889   Wins medal at Académie Julian; *Dreaming* and *Autumn* accepted in Salon, Paris; returns to Toronto from Paris; rents two large rooms on top story of Toronto Arcade Building for studio and living-quarters; begins painting *Mortgaging the Homestead*, *The Story*, and *The Other Side of the Question*

1890   Spring: *The Story* hangs in Salon, Paris; Reid elected full member, RCA, submits *Mortgaging the Homestead* as Diploma Picture; begins teaching at Central Ontario School of Art and Design (became Ontario College of Art) (until 1929); July: rents old mill as summer studio at Lampton Mills, Ontario, paints *The Berry Pickers*; Summer: Ontario School of Art re-organized by Ontario Department of Education, transferred from the Normal School Building to the new galleries of the OSA at 165 King St. W., Toronto; wins bronze medal of Central Canada Exposition Association; Fall: Central Ontario School of Art and Design opens, staffed by William Cruikshank, Robert Holmes and G.A. Reid; 29 November-12 December: one-man exhibition at Matthews Brothers and Co., Toronto, of work executed during summer of 1890

1891   Winter: Reid divides his tower studio in Toronto Arcade into two storeys, one for use as a private teaching studio; begins working on *Family Prayer*; Spring: *The Berry Pickers* exhibited at Salon, Paris, *Forbidden Fruit* at Philadelphia Museum; Summer: vacations in Catskills, upstate New York, for first time; Reids become members of Onteora Club, N.Y., spending summers at Onteora to 1917; December: *Exhibition of Paintings by G.A. Reid RCA and Mary Hiester Reid*, Art Association of Montreal

1892   To Onteora, builds cottage and studio, and executes first mural; Spring: *Lullaby* in Salon, Paris; December 13-14: auction of *Paintings by Mr. and Mrs. G.A. Reid* held at Oliver, Coate and Co., Toronto

1893   Reid visits World's Columbian Exposition, Chicago, wins bronze medal for *The Foreclosure of the Mortgage*; founder-member of the Palette Club, Toronto

1894   February: founder-member of Society of Mural Decorators, with six other artists devises scheme for mural decoration of Toronto City Hall; Spring: *A Modern Madonna* sent to Salon, Paris; conducts first summer painting class, Onteora; *The Foreclosure of the Mortgage* wins bronze medal at California Midwinter International Exposition, San Francisco; December: participates in six-artist exhibition of works in oil, watercolour and black-and-white at American Art Galleries, American Art Association, New York

1895   Designs Memorial Church, Onteora Park, New York

1896   To Paris for two months, then Spain; *Portrait* hangs in Salon, Paris; Reid copies Velasquez paintings in Prado, Madrid;

1897   Elected President, OSA (to 1901); founder-member, Toronto Guild of Civic Art; begins work on Toronto City Hall murals on his own initiative (completed 1899)

1900   Wins Central Canada Exhibition Association Medal, first prize for oil painting

1901   Founder-member, Canadian Society of Applied Art; appointed chairman of staff of Central Ontario School of Art and Design, Toronto

1902   March-April: first exhibition of the Society of Arts and Crafts, Toronto; July-October: to Scotland and London with M.H. Reid; Toronto Guild of Civic Art, with Reid as Convener, presents proposal for mural decoration of Ontario Legislative Building (no action taken, as proposal voted down by Legislature)

1903   Paints mural for Arts Building, Queen's University, Kingston

1904   Serves as RCA representative on committee preparing proposals for mural decoration of the rotunda of the Parliament Buildings, Ottawa, the key panel, *Ave Canada*, to have been painted by Reid; wins bronze medal for *Music* at St. Louis Universal Exposition

1905   Toronto Guild of Civic Art formally presents proposals for murals for Parliament Buildings, Ottawa

1906   Elected President, RCA (to 1907), begins organizing a series of special travelling RCA exhibitions;chairs committee for publication of Ontario Department of Education pamphlet for distribution to Ontario schools, giving a brief sketch of the movement for art education in public schools up to that time; September: begins construction of his new two-studio house, Upland Cottage, in Wychwood Park, Toronto; Winter: moves to Upland Cottage

1907   As president of the RCA, Reid launches movement for construction of a building and of hiring a director for the National Gallery of Canada and appointment of a director

1908   Advisory Arts Council established to serve as liaison between RCA and federal government; Reid paints historical pageants commemorating Quebec Tercentenary, Quebec City, completes first large historical subject, *The Arrival of Champlain at Quebec*

1910   To Scotland, England and Netherlands with M.H. Reid; on committee of Art Museum of Toronto, which obtains incorporation with design of establishing a permanent art gallery in Toronto

1911   Central Ontario School of Art and Industrial Design housed in Grange Park, Toronto

1912   Founder-member, the Associated Watercolour Painters, Toronto; appointed first Principal, Ontario College of Art (to 1929)

1913   *The Foreclosure of the Mortgage* exhibited at Royal Academy, London; Spring: Reid broaches idea to council of O.C.A. of inaugurating an outdoor summer art school for study of landscape, figure and animal painting, quarters obtained in York Mills for four-month session (school removed to Thornhill in 1918)

1915   Exhibit of paintings by G.A. and M.H. Reid held at Royal Ontario Museum, Toronto, in aid of Red Cross

1918   Commissioned to paint munitions workers in factories for Canadian War Records Commission; serves as honourary secretary of the

Council, Art Museum of Toronto; new building of Art Museum of Toronto open at Grange Park; Reids sell Onteora cottage

1919   Works as chief architect on new Ontario College of Art building, McCaul St., Toronto; *The Foreclosure of the Mortgage* destroyed by fire in warehouse, London, England

1920   21 September: cornerstone of new OCA building laid; Art Museum of Toronto becomes Art Gallery of Toronto

1921   30 September: new OCA building, designed by Reid, officially opened; 4 October: death of Mary Hiester Reid, Toronto

1922   Reid finds quarters for summer art school of OCA at Port Hope, Ontario

1923:   December: marries Mary Wrinch Reid, Toronto artist

1923-24 Travels to United States, Scotland, England, France, Belgium, Netherlands, to conduct survey of art schools, revisits Pennsylvania Academy and Académie Julian

1925   Summer: first painting trip to Algoma, with M.W. Reid; designs two small studio houses on Alcina Avenue, Wychwood Park, Toronto; Fall: wins RCA commission to execute decorative murals for Earlscourt Public Library, Toronto

1926   August: painting trip to Quebec, with M.W. Reid; becomes founder-member of Canadian Society of Painters in Water Colour

1928   Begins Canadian history murals for Jarvis Collegiate, Toronto (completed 1930); August: first painting trip to Temagami

1929   Retires as Principal from OCA, replaced by J.E.H. MacDonald; Fall: painting trip to Abitibi Canyon, Ontario, with M.W. Reid

1934   Begins work on murals for Paleontology Gallery, Royal Ontario Museum, Toronto (completed 1938); paints replicas of *The Foreclosure of the Mortgage* and *The Homeseekers*

1938   *Logging* presented to Government of Canada for hanging in Canada House, London, by Brig.-Gen. Sweny, G.M.C., D.S.O.

1942   G.A. Reid Collection (c. 400 works) presented to Government of Ontario for hanging in Ontario Legislative Building, Toronto, and Ontario schools

1945	16 January: dinner in honour of Reid held at Art Gallery of Toronto
1947	23 August: death of G.A. Reid, Toronto
1948	March: memorial exhibition held at Art Gallery of Toronto, in association with OSA 76th Annual Exhibition

Catalogue of the Exhibition

Key:
 * Shown at Toronto, Thunder Bay, Kitchener, Burlington
** Shown at Toronto only

1

Medals awarded to George A. Reid

(a) Ontario School of Art President's
Medal 1880
Silver
4.7 cm dia.

(b) Colonial and Indian Exhibition
Medal 1886
Bronze
5.1 cm dia.

(c) Central Canada Exhibition Association Medal First Prize for Oil
Painting, 1890
Bronze
4.2 cm

(d) World's Columbian Exposition
Medal 1892-93
Bronze
7.6 cm dia.

(e) California Midwinter International
Exposition Medal 1894
Bronze
6.4 x 6 cm

(f) St. Louis Universal Exposition
Medal 1904
Bronze
6.4 cm dia.

Art Gallery of Ontario, Gift of Mrs. K.
Hallam, Toronto, 1970

2
The Newsboy (copy after Robert Harris) 1880
Oil on board
49.0 x 33.8 cm
Confederation Centre Art Gallery and Museum Permanent Collection, Charlottetown

*3
Study after Antique Cast, the
Borghese Warrior, Philadelphia 1884
Pen-and-ink on paper
16.7 x 10.1 cm
Art Gallery of Ontario, Gift of Mary
Wrinch Reid to the E.P. Taylor Refer-
ence Library, 1957, Transferred to
the permanent collection, 1986

4
Study of a Young Man Done in the
Academy of Fine Arts, Philadelphia
[Charles Grafly] 1882-84
Oil on paper
16.4 x 9.5 cm
Art Gallery of Ontario, Gift of Mary
Wrinch Reid to the E.P. Taylor Refer-
ence Library, 1957, Transferred to
the painting collection, 1982

5
Philadelphia Academy Life Study
1882-84
Oil on thin board
29.7 x 13.2 cm
Art Gallery of Ontario, Gift of Mary
Wrinch Reid to the E.P. Taylor Reference Library, 1957, Transferred to
the painting collection, 1982

6
*Study of a Woman with arms on
head done at the Academy of Fine
Arts, Philadelphia*   1884
Oil on paper
18.6 x 9.5 cm
Art Gallery of Ontario, Gift of Mary
Wrinch Reid to the E.P. Taylor Reference Library, 1957, Transferred to
the painting collection, 1982

NOTE: Reproduced in colour on
page 20.

7
Self Portrait 1884
Oil on cardboard
15.9 x 13.3
Art Gallery of Ontario, Gift of the
Reuben Wells Leonard Estate, 1966

**8
Portrait of Mary Hiester Reid 1885
Oil on canvas
76.8 x 64.1 cm
National Gallery of Canada, Ottawa,
Gift of Mrs. George A. Reid, Toronto,
1965

9
Head of a Nun   1885
Oil on board
30.5 x 25.4 cm
Government of Ontario Art Collection,
Toronto

10
Street Scene, Malaga, Spain   1885
Oil on canvas
36.6 x 26.4 cm
Kaspar Gallery, Toronto

11
Adam Reid   1886
Oil on canvas board
61.0 x 50.8 cm
London Regional Art Gallery, Gift of
Mrs. G.A. Reid, 1955

12
The Call to Dinner   1886-87
Oil on canvas
161.6 x 219.8 cm
McMaster University Art Gallery,
Hamilton, Presented by Moulton
College, 1954; Presented to Moulton
College by Mr. and Mrs. J.H.L. Patterson

13
At the Window   1888
Oil on canvas
81.0 x 102.0 cm
Collection of Glenbow Museum,
Calgary, Alberta

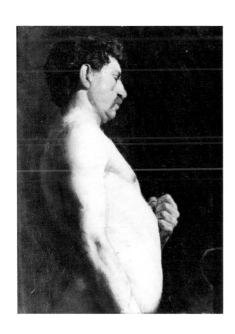

14
Nude Study   1888
Oil on canvas
29.8 x 22.9 cm
Art Gallery of Ontario, Gift of Mary
Wrinch Reid, 1957

15
Nude Study
Oil on canvas
40.0 x 30.5 cm
Art Gallery of Ontario, Gift of William
A. Drake, Roche's Point, Ontario

16
Study of Head and Torso   1889
Oil on canvas board
50.8 x 35.6 cm
London Regional Art Gallery, Gift of
Mrs. G.A. Reid, 1950

17
A Life Study   1889
Oil on board
31.1 x 21.8 cm
Government of Ontario Art Collection,
Toronto

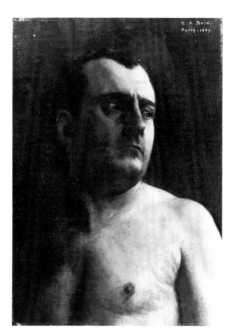
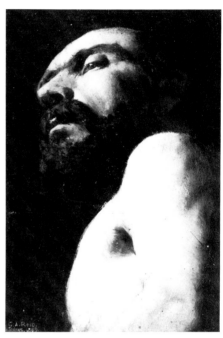

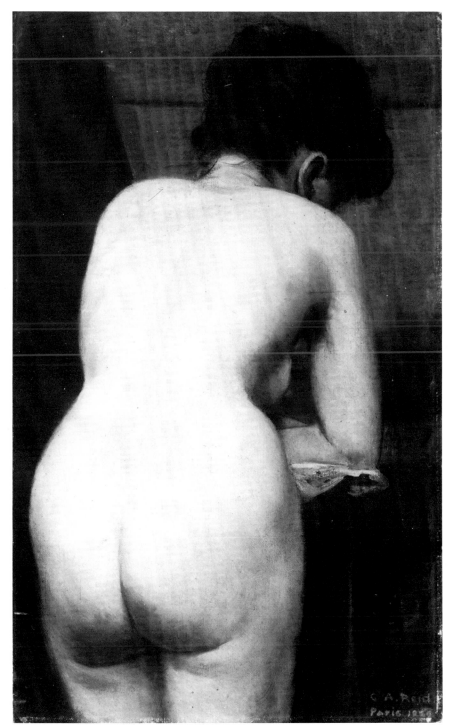

19
*Study Portrait in the Colarossi
Academy, Paris* 1889
Oil on canvas
31.6 x 26.6 cm
Art Gallery of Ontario, Gift of Mary
Wrinch Reid to the E.P. Taylor Refer-
ence Library, Transferred to the
painting collection, 1982

18
Nude Leaning on a Stool 1889
Oil on canvas board
55.9 X 35.6 cm
London Regional Art Gallery, Gift of
Mrs. G.A. Reid, 1950

20
Job, Composition, Julian Academy
1888-89
Oil on paper
21.9 x 36.3 cm
Art Gallery of Ontario, Gift of Mary
Wrinch Reid to the E.P. Taylor Reference Library, 1957, Transferred to
the painting collection, 1982

21
*The Sword of Damocles, Julian
Academy*   1888-89
Oil on canvas
25.5 x 39.9 cm
Art Gallery of Ontario, Gift of Mary
Wrinch Reid to the E.P. Taylor Refer-
ence Library, 1957, Transferred to
the painting collection, 1982

22
Composition, Julian Academy, Paris
[Hannibal crossing the Alps]   1888-89
Oil on canvas
24.0 x 32.1 cm
Art Gallery of Ontario, Gift of Mary
Wrinch Reid to the E.P. Taylor Reference Library, 1957, Transferred to
the painting collection, 1982

23
Cluny Museum, Paris   1888
Oil on paper
14.4 x 11.4 cm
Art Gallery of Ontario, Gift of Mary
Wrinch Reid to the E.P. Taylor Reference Library, 1957, Transferred to
the painting collection, 1982

24
Cluny Museum, Paris   1888
Oil on paper
17.1 x 14.6 cm
Art Gallery of Ontario, Gift of Mary
Wrinch Reid to the E.P. Taylor Reference Library, 1957, Transferred to
the painting collection, 1982

25
Cluny Museum, Paris   1888
Oil on paper
23.0 x 15.4 cm
Art Gallery of Ontario, Gift of Mary
Wrinch Reid to the E.P. Taylor Reference Library, 1957, Transferred to
the painting collection, 1982

*26
Notre-Dame, Paris   1888
Pen-and-ink on paper
11.1 x 17.7 cm
Art Gallery of Ontario, Gift of Mary
Wrinch Reid to the E.P. Taylor Refer-
ence Library, 1957, Transferred to
the permanent collection, 1986

27
Notre-Dame, Paris   1888
Oil on panel
22.9 x 33.9 cm
Art Gallery of Ontario, Purchased
with funds made available from the
Estate of Margaret L. Thomas,
Toronto, 1984

NOTE: Reproduced in colour on
page 24.

28 (A)
Pen-and-ink study for *Logging* I   1888
Pen-and-ink on paper
17.6 x 10.5 cm
Art Gallery of Ontario, Gift of Mary
Wrinch Reid to the E.P. Taylor Refer-
ence Library, 1957, Transferred to
the permanent collection, 1986

28 (B)
Pen-and-ink study for *Logging* II   1888
Pen-and-ink on paper
17.6 x 10.5 cm
Art Gallery of Ontario, Gift of Mary
Wrinch Reid to the E.P. Taylor Refer-
ence Library, 1957, Transferred to
the permanent collection, 1986

29
Pen-and-ink study for *Logging*
III   1888
Pen-and-ink on paper
9.5 x 17.7 cm
Art Gallery of Ontario, Gift of Mary
Wrinch Reid to the E.P. Taylor Refer-
ence Library, 1957, Transferred to
the permanent collection, 1986

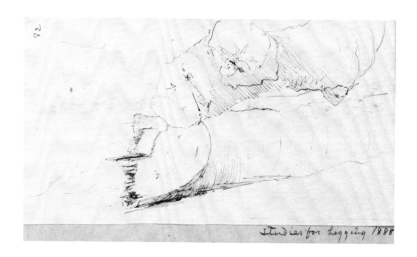

30 (A)
First oil sketch for *Logging*   1888
Oil on paper
6.3 x 12.9 cm
Art Gallery of Ontario, Gift of Mary
Wrinch Reid to the E.P. Taylor Refer-
ence Library, 1957, Transferred to
the permanent collection, 1986

30 (B)
Second oil study for *Logging*   1888
Oil on paper
6.3 x 12.8 cm
Art Gallery of Ontario, Gift of Mary
Wrinch Reid to the E.P. Taylor Reference Library, 1957, Transferred to
the permanent collection, 1986

31
Head of a Man   1889
Oil on panel
17.8 x 15.9 cm
The National Gallery of Canada,
Ottawa

32
Photograph of *Logging*   1889
Oil on canvas
111.7 x 183.0 cm
Department of External Affairs,
Canada/Ministère des affaires
extérieures du Canada, Ottawa

33
Study in the Park   1889
Oil on board
6.9 x 9.8 cm
Art Gallery of Hamilton, Gift of Mr.
and Mrs. J.A. McCuaig, 1966

34
Forbidden Fruit   1889
Oil on canvas
77.8 x 122.9 cm
Art Gallery of Hamilton, Gift of the
Women's Committee, 1960

35
Study for *The Story*   1889
Oil on board
25.4 x 35.6 cm
Private Collection

36
The Story   1890
Oil on canvas
123.0 x 164.3 cm
Collection of the Winnipeg Art
Gallery, donation from the Hugh F.
Osler Estate

37
The Other Side of the Question   1890
Oil on canvas
104.0 x 132.5 cm
Art Gallery of Ontario, Purchase,
1985

NOTE: Reproduced in colour on
page 28

38
Study for *Mortgaging the Homestead*
1890
Oil on canvas
27.9 x 43.2 cm
Government of Ontario Art Collection, Toronto

39
Photograph of *Mortgaging the Homestead* 1890
Oil on canvas
128.3 x 212.1 cm
The National Gallery of Canada, Ottawa, Royal Canadian Academy of Arts Diploma Work, deposited 1890

**40
Family Prayer   1890
Oil on canvas
101.5 x 127.0 cm
Victoria University, University of
Toronto

41
Family Prayer   1892
Oil on board
25.5 x 30.48 cm
Private Collection

42
The Berry Pickers   1890
Oil on canvas
167.7 x 127.0 cm
Government of Ontario Art Collection, Toronto

NOTE: Reproduced in colour on front cover

43
Mother and Baby   ca. 1890
Oil on board
19.1 x 15.2 cm
Art Gallery of Ontario, Gift of Mary
Wrinch Reid, 1957

44
Mrs. Parker, Onteora   1892
Oil on paper
17.8 x 12.2 cm
Art Gallery of Ontario, Gift of Mary
Wrinch Reid to the E.P. Taylor Refer-
ence Library, 1957, Transferred to
the painting collection, 1982

**45
First sketch for *The Foreclosure of
the Mortgage*,   1893
Charcoal and pencil on paper
9.7 x 13.9 cm
Art Gallery of Ontario, Gift of Mary
Wrinch Reid to the E.P. Taylor Reference Library, 1957, Transferred to
the permanent collection, 1986

46
The Foreclosure of the Mortgage
1892
Oil on board
16.8 x 25.4 cm
The National Gallery of Canada,
Bequest of the Estate of Robert Burn
Bond

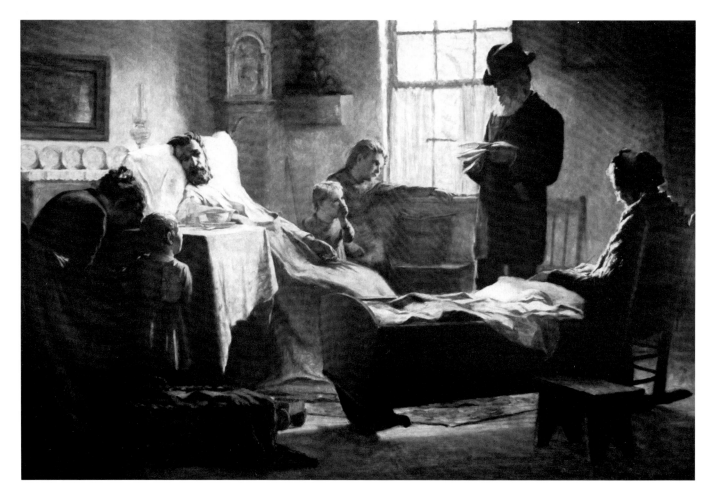

47
Photograph of *The Foreclosure of the
Mortgage* 1934
(Replica of original canvas dated
1893, destroyed in fire in 1919)
Oil on canvas
180.3 x 276.9 cm
Government of Ontario Art Collec-
tion, Toronto

48
Tending the Baby   1893
oil on card
30.0 x 23.5 cm
Mr. and Mrs. J. Browning, Toronto

49
*Copy after Velasquez - Portrait of a
Dwarf with a Dog*   1896
Oil on canvas
137.0 x 102.0 cm
The National Gallery of Canada,
Ottawa

50
Nude Study   1896
Oil on canvas
60.1 x 45.7 cm
London Regional Art Gallery, Gift of
Mrs. G.A. Reid, 1950

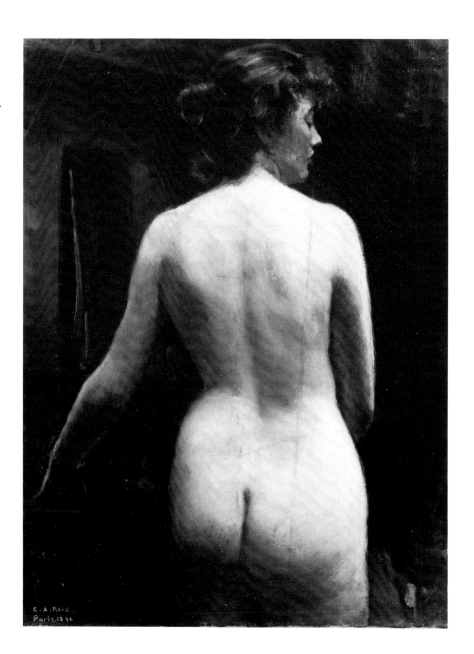

51
Portrait, Mary Hiester Reid 1898
Oil on canvas
76.8 x 64.1 cm
Art Gallery of Ontario, Gift of Mary
Wrinch Reid, 1954

52
Seated Nude Study 1898
Oil on canvas
73.7 x 38.1 cm
London Regional Art Gallery, Gift of
Mrs. G.A. Reid, 1950

53
Music 1910
Painted plaster
34.9 x 11.5 cm
Art Gallery of Windsor, Gift of Gordon
Conn, 1973

**54
Study for Decorative Panel, Music
1900
Pastel on cardboard
40.3 x 14.5 cm
Art Gallery of Ontario, Gift of Mary
Wrinch Reid, 1954

NOTE: Reproduced in colour on
page 32

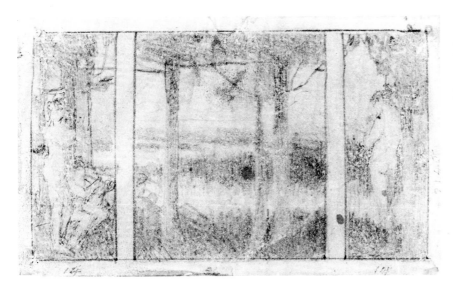

*55
Composition, Music 1899
Pencil on paper
13.6 x 18.2 cm
Art Gallery of Ontario, Gift of Mary
Wrinch Reid to the E.P. Taylor Refer-
ence Library, 1957, Transferred to
the painting collection, 1982

56
Music   1900
Oil on canvas
229.3 x 69.5 cm
Government of Ontario Art Collec-
tion, Toronto

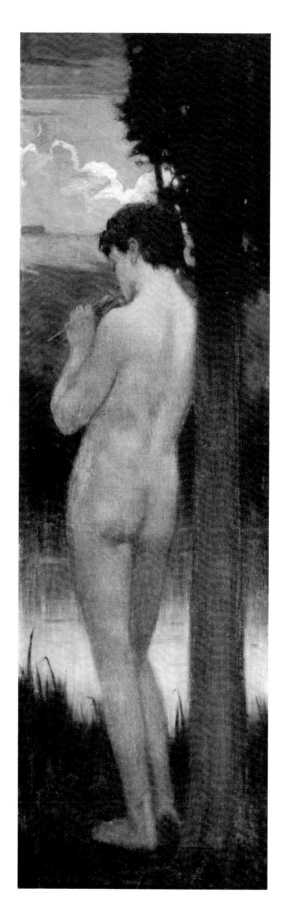